FREQUENTLY ASKED

Questions
About the Saguaro

Janice Emily Bowers

Western National Parks Association
Tucson, Arizona

How is "saguaro" pronounced?

Say "saw-WAH-row," with the accent on the middle syllable. The word is probably a Hispanicized version of a Native word for this plant.

saw-WAH-row

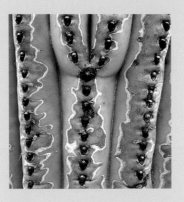

What is a saguaro?

The saguaro is a cactus that belongs to the plant family Cactaceae. Cacti are distinguished by several traits, including succulent branches and clustered spines produced from circular patches called areoles. Saguaros belong to the subfamily Cactoideae, and within that subfamily to the tribe Pachycereae. The larger members of the Cactoideae, including the saguaro, are called columnar cacti because of their tall, cylindrical stems.

Is the saguaro the only columnar cactus in the United States?

There are two other species of columnar cacti in southern Arizona. The organ pipe cactus (above left) branches profusely from the base and can grow to a height of 26 feet. The senita, or old man cactus, has a similar growth form and reaches 10 feet. Both cacti are common in Organ Pipe Cactus National Monument near the Arizona-Mexico border. A few more kinds of columnar cacti grow in Florida.

Where do saguaros grow?

The saguaro is limited to the Sonoran Desert. It is common throughout the desert in Arizona and in the western half of Sonora, Mexico. In California, populations are sparse and found only near the Arizona border.

What restricts their geographic distribution?

The northern and northeastern limits of saguaros lie where subfreezing temperatures last for more than twenty-four hours. Cold limits their growth at higher elevations as well, and few are found above 5,000 feet. Because saguaros need warmth and ample moisture for seed germination, their western limit lies where summer rains become scanty and infrequent. In Mexico, saguaros drop out as desert gives way to thornscrub. In these dense woodlands, saguaro seedlings lose out in the fierce competition for space, water, and soil nutrients.

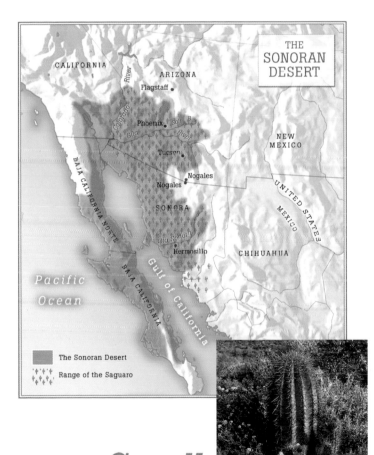

How many saguaros are there?

A rough estimate of the saguaro population can be made from the density of saguaros across their range (500 to 50,000 plants per square mile) and the size of the Sonoran Desert in the United States and Mexico (120,000 square miles). At least 55 percent of this area is uninhabited by saguaros. Another 10 percent is devoted to towns, cities, and irrigated agriculture. The total population of saguaros in the remainder of the Sonoran Desert is likely more than 20 million and probably less than 2 billion. The human population of the Sonoran Desert is about 6 million.

Small saguaro plants can tolerate some nighttime frost as long as temperatures rise above freezing the next day.

How big does a saguaro get?

Through the years, this has been a much-debated topic. This year's champion could be gone next year, making it hard to verify reports of the tallest plant ever. A saguaro that reportedly measured 59 feet in 1991 has since fallen, for example. Although saguaros can exceed 50 feet in height, this is unusual. Most plants do not grow much taller than 30 feet. This is big for a cactus, but not for a tree; conifers such as Douglas fir and white fir commonly reach 300 feet.

How fast do saguaros grow?

It depends. Small saguaros grow very slowly. At the end of their first year, seedlings are no more than one-quarter inch in height. After another four years, they might be a full inch. As the plants gain in volume and surface area, increasing their capacity to produce sugars and store water, their rate of growth accelerates. Just before saguaros reach reproductive size—about six to twelve feet tall in the Tucson area—they are growing their fastest, at about five inches per year. Reproduction diverts energy to flowers and fruits at the expense of growth in height, so the rate of growth declines sharply when plants are big enough to bloom. The appearance of branches halts this downward trend. As a source of additional sugars, branches compensate for the energy drain of flowering and fruiting. Once branching begins, the growth rate levels off at two or three inches a year.

Is the saguaro the tallest cactus in the world?

Many other columnar cacti equal or exceed the saguaro in height. In South America, at least three species reach 40 feet and another four get to 50 feet. In Mexico, at least six species are about 40 feet at maximum height, five are about 50 feet, and one can reach 80 feet.

Most growth *occurs during the* **summer rainy season,** *and at any location plants grow more in a wet summer than in a dry one.*

Why are saguaros skinny some times and fat other times?

The outside of a saguaro is fluted like an accordion with alternating ribs and furrows that allow the plant to expand and contract. (These ribs, made of fleshy cortex tissue, are not to be confused with the woody ribs inside the plant.) Saguaros expand as they take up rainwater from the soil. Whatever water they do not use for growth they store in the cortex. During dry seasons, they use some of this water to live and lose some by transpiration. As they lose their moisture, the stems contract.

What holds up these huge, heavy plants?

Just as human beings are suspended from an internal structure of bones, saguaros are hung upon an internal structure of wooden rods, about thirty in the trunk and a dozen in each branch. The rods, usually called ribs, are arranged in a circle, forming a cylinder. Inside the cylinder is pith; outside is a thick band of cortex, a specialized tissue that stores carbohydrates and water. After a plant dies, its fleshy tissues rot away, exposing the ribs. Although the wood looks spongy and weak, the sum of the ribs is greater than their individual parts. The cylindrical arrangement provides strength and flexibility, allowing plants to sway slightly in the wind while sustaining heavy loads without buckling.

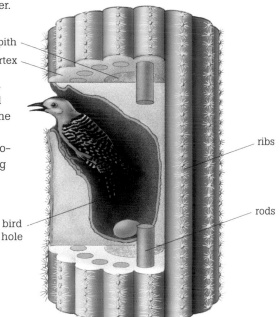

pith
cortex
ribs
rods
bird hole

How much do saguaros weigh?

Given the volume of any saguaro, we can estimate its weight from two simple facts: A quart of water weighs 2.2 pounds, and about 94 percent of the weight of a saguaro is water. A 20-foot-tall saguaro without branches has an estimated volume of about 960 quarts. The weight of 960 quarts of water is 2,112 pounds, so a 20-foot plant likely weighs about a ton, as much as a full-grown American bison.

A tall plant with **several branches** *might weigh as much as* **eight tons.**

How old are saguaros?

We can age saguaros according to height. The relation between height and age varies with climate, among other factors. In the Tucson area, a plant five feet in height is about 30 to 40 years old. A 20-foot-tall plant is likely to be around 70 to 90 years. The tallest saguaros might be about 200 years in age. Most plants do not live past an age of 150 or so.

	Estimated Rainfall		
	Saguaro N.P. Rincon Mt. District	Saguaro N.P. Tucson Mt. District	Organ Pipe Cactus N.M.
Elevation	3100'-4500'	2650'-4600'	1670'-4700'
Average Summer Rainfall	5.29"	4.44"	4.02"
Average Yearly Rainfall	12.30"	10.27"	7.56"

	Estimated Age		
	Saguaro N.P. Rincon Mt. District	Saguaro N.P. Tucson Mt. District	Organ Pipe Cactus N.M.
Height			
1 foot	17 years	23 years	31 years
5	32	44	62
10	45	59	81
15	56	72	97
20	68	86	113
25	82	103	133
30	97	122	156
35	116	147	163
40	138	180	194
45	167	223	no data

How does climate affect growth?

Growth varies with climate. Plants at Organ Pipe Cactus National Monument grow more slowly than those at the Tucson Mountain District of Saguaro National Park, which in turn grow more slowly than those at the Rincon Mountain District of the Park.

How deep are their roots?

Saguaros have an extensive system of lateral roots that radiate up to 50 feet from the trunk and lie within five inches of the soil surface. The broad, shallow root system harvests soil moisture from a wide area, taking advantage of light rains that do not penetrate deeply into the ground.

Where are the "baby" saguaros?

There are more than you might think. A survey in the Rincon Mountain District of Saguaro National Park found that 77 to 85 percent of saguaros in the population were no more than three feet tall, that is, aged 20 years or younger. Small saguaros mostly grow where they are protected from frost, sun, and hungry animals—thus you find them sheltered by trees and shrubs, tucked among rocks and grass clumps, and poking up amidst fallen branches. A careful search is necessary to discover well-hidden plants no larger than a Ping-Pong ball.

When do branches first appear?

Branching starts once saguaros are about 15 feet tall.

What determines where the branches appear?

The first branches appear about 11 or 12 feet above the ground, more or less where plants reach their maximum girth. Some observers think that placement of branches around the trunk is more or less random; others believe that saguaros branch most profusely toward the south. Branches some-times appear just below the site of frost damage or some other injury.

How many branches will a saguaro develop?

The faster a plant grows, the more branches it is likely to have. Most plants do not develop more than 10 to 20 branches. Fast growth is associated with wetter climates, thus saguaros at Saguaro National Park average more branches per plant than those at Organ Pipe Cactus National Monument. In the driest locations, even the oldest plants might never branch.

Why do they branch?

The more branches a saguaro has, the more fruits and seeds it can produce. As the number of seeds goes up, so does the chance that at least a few will germinate, grow to maturity, and reproduce in their turn.

Saguaros with as many as 40 to 50 branches are rare.

Why do some branches point downwards?

When saguaro tissue freezes, the cells are damaged and can no longer hold water. As a result, the tissue loses its normal turgidity. If frost damage occurs where a branch attaches to the trunk, the attachment point becomes mushy, allowing the branch to droop.

What are the constrictions on saguaro trunks?

Frost damage to a growing tip causes the most pronounced constrictions, which look almost as if someone had wrapped a strong wire around the stem. If the damage is not lethal, growth slows or stops for a time and then continues above the point of injury. Annual growth increments produce faint constrictions. These are spaced more or less regularly from the bottom to the top of the plant, giving the trunk a wavy appearance.

Crests can be regular and **fanlike,** *or irregular and incongruous.*

What are those strange, fanlike growths on some saguaros?

Occasionally the main trunk and upper stems of a saguaro fuse and grow together as a single unit or bundle. The Latin word for bundle is "fascia," thus such saguaros are said to be fasciated. These plants are also described as "crested." The ultimate cause of fasciation is unknown. Many kinds of plants, not just saguaros, can become fasciated.

What time of day do saguaros flower?

Saguaro flowers open between 10 p.m. and midnight and close by late afternoon of the following day, never to open again.

What time of year do saguaros flower?

The flowering season is typically April through June. Although most plants flower only in late spring, a small number of oddball individuals bloom in the summer. Rarely, a few flowers appear in other months, even in winter.

When do saguaros bloom for the first time?

Flowers first appear when plants reach a height of six to 12 feet—about 35 to 70 years of age, depending on location.

What color are the flowers?

Saguaro flowers are white, and measure three to four inches in width and length. They are funnel-shaped. The many petals are fused at the base to form a tube that contains abundant nectar. Numerous stamens, the male reproductive organs, line the tube and surround the opening of the funnel. The female reproductive organ, the pistil, comprises an ovary and a threadlike style that splits at the top into several stigmas. Inside the ovary are a few thousand ovules, or unfertilized seeds.

How many flowers and fruits does a saguaro produce?

When it blooms for the first time, a saguaro puts out half a dozen flowers but may yield only one or two ripe fruits. Fecundity increases as the plant grows, and by the time it is almost tall enough to branch, its single stem might yield as many as 100 fruits. Branching increases flower and fruit production still further.

How are the flowers pollinated?

Pollination is the transfer of pollen from stamens, the male reproductive organ, to pistils, the female reproductive organ. Pollen grains fertilize ovules, which then develop into seeds. Saguaro flowers are self-incompatible—pollen from another plant is necessary for fertilization. Because saguaro pollen is too heavy to be blown from plant to plant by wind, animals must move it.

petals

style

stigma

stamens

nectar

scales

ovary

Do saguaro flowers have an odor?

Their fragrance has been compared to that of an overripe melon. Saguaros, like many other kinds of columnar cacti, are sometimes pollinated by nectar-feeding bats, which have learned that musky, fruity odors often indicate the presence of abundant nectar. The nectar in saguaro flowers is an important food source for these bats and a delicious dietary supplement for at least nine species of birds.

What about the red flowers in summertime?

Those are not flowers. When ripe, the fig-shaped fruits split wide open, revealing scarlet lobes that look like petals from a distance.

Which animals pollinate saguaros?

The many animals drawn to saguaro flowers for nectar include lesser long-nosed bat, honeybee, various native bees, white-lined sphinx moth, and a number of birds, among them white-winged dove, mourning dove, Costa's hummingbird, Gila woodpecker, curve-bill thrasher, verdin, gilded flicker, and house finch. Doves, woodpeckers, and bats plunge their heads deeply into the blossoms when foraging for nectar. Thickly dusted with pollen on their head and shoulders, they then visit flowers on neighboring plants, depositing some pollen and picking up more. Bees pollinate many blossoms as well.

Despite heavy visitation, about 40 to 50 percent of saguaro flowers never set fruit.

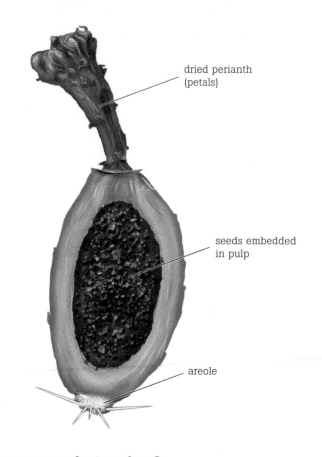

dried perianth (petals)

seeds embedded in pulp

areole

How many seeds does a saguaro plant produce?

A saguaro fruit contains 2,000 to 2,500 tiny, black seeds. An average plant produces about 150 fruits annually, or 300,000 to 375,000 seeds per year.

When does the fruit ripen?

In June and July. Fruits turn purplish red as they ripen. Generally, fruits ripen and disperse seeds just in time for the first heavy rains of summer.

Why so many seeds?

The large number of seeds compensates for the high mortality of seeds and seedlings. Saguaros need heavy summer rains—at least one and one-half inches over two or three days—for germination. If summer rains are delayed or sparse, the entire seed crop is likely to be consumed by ants, birds, rodents, and other animals before it has a chance to germinate. New seedlings face severe hazards from consumption by rodents or rabbits to death by frost or drought, and fewer than 1 percent survive as long as 12 months.

Over its **reproductive lifetime** *a large saguaro might shed as many as 40 million seeds.*

Is the fruit edible?

The seeds are embedded in a sweet, succulent pulp reminiscent of strawberries. There isn't much of it, but what there is tastes delicious and is highly sought after by many animals. The thick rind around the mass of seeds is rather tough and not especially flavorful.

Large paloverde, ironwood, and mesquite "nurse trees" can harbor anywhere from one to a dozen saguaros.

What happens to the fruits and seeds?

After ripe fruits split open, they typically remain on the plant for a short while, giving birds first crack at the seeds. Once fruits drop to the ground, seeds are avidly foraged by a wide variety of animals, including harvester ants, ground squirrels, coyotes, javelina, rabbits, woodrats, kangaroo rats, and mice. The digestive processes of ants, doves, and mouse-sized rodents generally destroy the seeds. Larger mammals are more apt to pass some seeds unharmed through the digestive tract. Birds other than doves also pass some intact seeds, often when perched on tree branches. Saguaro seeds deposited under trees get a good start in life. The canopy of the tree, which is sometimes called a "nurse tree," protects seedlings from excessively high and low temperatures, and the litter of twigs on the ground helps hide them from animals.

What causes those round holes in the trunks and branches?

Two kinds of birds, Gila woodpeckers and gilded flickers, drill nest holes in saguaro trunks and branches. Gila woodpeckers make the smaller holes, flickers make the larger ones. Gila woodpeckers (right) drill nest holes from within a few feet of the saguaro apex down to about 15 feet above the ground. The cavities they make are small enough to be contained within the cortex of the stem and are not harmful to the plant.

Because gilded flickers need large nests, you might expect them to drill where saguaro stems are widest. The flicker skull is poorly suited to excavating hard wood, however, so flickers work near the top of the saguaro where the woody ribs are new and soft. This is also where the stems are relatively narrow, so narrow in fact that the entire nest cannot be contained within the cortex. Flickers must drill through the cortex into the pith, severing the ribs. This weakens the structural integrity of the stem, which starts to bend at the point of injury and eventually snaps off.

Where flickers are common,
topless saguaros
are often common, too.

Do other animals use these holes?

You bet. Good nest holes are at a premium in a place where big trees are few. Saguaro holes make particularly good nest sites because they are insulated by the surrounding cactus tissue, which keeps the nests cooler in summer and warmer in winter. They are also inaccessible to many predators. After woodpeckers and flickers abandon their nest holes, other cavity-nesting birds quickly move in. These borrowers include ash-throated and brown-crested flycatcher; elf, ferruginous pygmy, and western screech owl; purple martin; American kestrel; house sparrow; and starling.

What is a saguaro boot?

Saguaros respond to injury by secreting callus tissue. The secretion molds itself to the shape of the injury, whether a deep hole made by a woodpecker or a shallow tunnel made by a moth caterpillar. Callus tissue hardens into a corklike layer that remains in place through the life of the plant, protecting it from invasion by bacteria and fungi. When plants die and rot, the callus tissue falls out. Some resemble boots; others look more like bottles, buttons, or balls.

Do other birds build nests in saguaros?
No other birds drill holes, but cactus wrens and doves sometimes construct nests in the crotches formed by branches
and trunks, and red-tailed (left) and Harris hawks pile sticks
between branches to form their broad platform nests.

Why do saguaros have spines?
Anatomically speaking, a spine is a (greatly) modified leaf. In one sense, then, saguaros have
spines because they do not have leaves. In practical terms, spines probably serve several
functions. First, they offer some protection from browsing animals. Second, a combination of
dense spines and wool on the apex of each saguaro stem acts like a blanket on cold nights,
helping prevent frost injury to the tender growing tip. Finally, the network of spines along
the stems casts enough shade to protect the skin from sunburn. Old saguaros that have lost
many spines are subject to overheating of the surface tissues, especially on the south side of
the plant. The trunk then becomes discolored, a condition known as "epidermal browning."
The condition is not fatal.

How has the saguaro adapted to desert conditions?
The phenomenal water-storage capacity of the trunk keeps the plant alive during severe drought.
The waxy coating on the skin prevents undue moisture loss. The absence of leaves also circumvents
water loss. The green skin takes on the function of leaves, turning carbon dioxide from the atmos-
phere into the sugars needed for growth and reproduction.

Jackrabbits and packrats
are not easily deterred by spines and will
gnaw at cacti to get at the moist tissue inside.

Dramatic *fluctuations* in the size and age of *saguaro* populations are apparently normal.

I have heard that all the saguaros are dying. Is this true?

In a word, no. During the first part of the twentieth century, several carefully conducted studies suggested that saguaro populations in the Tucson area were declining. These populations had a preponderance of large, old plants and a marked scarcity of small, young ones, indicating that old plants would not be replaced as they reached the end of their natural lifespan. The prospect for saguaros looked grim. In the last part of the twentieth century, however, surveys of the same populations have revealed a dramatic turnaround, and in places where old plants are now scarce, young ones are common.

What causes the death of saguaros?

Small plants are vulnerable to seasonal aridity and frost. Rodents, rabbits, and other animals eat them. Cattle or other large animals may trample them. Adult plants can be killed by catastrophic freezes when nighttime temperatures drop to 21 degrees F or lower. Several years might pass before a severely frost-damaged saguaro actually dies from the event. Lightning strikes kill some saguaros, and strong winds uproot others, especially when the soil is saturated. Fire is deadly, although charred plants might continue to stand and even bloom for a few years after being burned.

Mature saguaros are well able to survive seasonal aridity, but they are not immune to drought, and during prolonged rainless periods, many small plants and even some large ones are apt to die.

Why do many saguaros seem to be the same size?

Seedlings become established infrequently; yet when conditions are right for establishment, a huge crop of young plants can take hold. The new cohort matures, reaches old age, and dies more or less in concert. As long as there are a few good establishment years every century, populations are likely to persist indefinitely. Although the magnificent saguaro forests of the past have disappeared in some locations, the current abundance of young plants promises that our grandchildren and great-grandchildren will get to walk through dense stands of saguaros some day.

What is the blackish fluid I sometimes see on saguaros? Does that mean they're dying?

Bacterial necrosis can overtake damaged tissue, creating pockets of rot that discharge blackish fluids down the trunk. Bacterial necrosis is not a cause of death but rather is the natural decay of tissues that are already dead or dying from frost damage, incompletely sealed wounds, or old age. After a catastrophic freeze in 1937, large numbers of saguaros in the Tucson area exhibited bacterial necrosis, leading researchers to conclude mistakenly that the plants were suffering from a deadly disease and that the saguaro was on the brink of extinction.

Can cities and saguaros coexist?

Even though builders are required by law to salvage saguaros that grow in the way of new construction projects, about half the transplants do not survive. More serious than the loss of individual plants is the wholesale obliteration of suitable habitat. Given good summer rains and plentiful seed crops, saguaro populations can rebound from drastic declines as long as their habitat remains intact.

Do exotic plants harm saguaros?

Yes. The proliferation of exotic plants does harm them; particularly harmful are red brome, an annual grass from the Mediterranean region, and buffelgrass, a perennial grass from southern Africa. Both species ignite easily when dry, and they grow in dense stands that rapidly carry fire across the desert. After wildfires, red brome regenerates from seed. Buffelgrass comes back quickly because, like most perennial grasses, it sprouts from underground buds. Saguaros, along with many other desert plants, are killed outright by wildfires and are slow to return to burned areas.

Even the most **favorable** **weather** *is of no benefit when* **seeds** *fall not on desert soil but on concrete or asphalt.*

How do Native peoples use the saguaro?

The O'odham collect fruits as they ripen, often in a race with birds. Native people use a long pole made from saguaro ribs lashed end to end to knock the fruits off the stems. They eat fresh fruits out of hand or boil them to make jam and syrup. They also grind the seeds into a nutritious flour and reconstitute the dried pulp in water for sweet drinks. The O'odham consume saguaro wine, made from fermented syrup, during a ceremony meant to encourage summer rains.

Are saguaros protected?

Arizona's native plant protection law protects all cacti, including saguaros, on public and private lands. Without a special permit from the state (for public lands) and explicit permission from the owner (for private lands), you may not destroy, dig up, mutilate, collect, cut, or harvest saguaros of any size. The prohibition includes flowers, fruits, seeds, and ribs.

What is the scientific name of the saguaro?

Carnegiea gigantea—*Carnegiea* after Andrew Carnegie (1835–1919), the steel baron and philanthropist, *gigantea* for the saguaro's impressive size. Andrew Carnegie founded the Carnegie Institution of Washington in 1902 to encourage research and discovery in a broad array of disciplines. Among the many projects funded by the Institution was a study of the Cactaceae by two taxonomists, Joseph Rose and Nathaniel Britton. Their decision to name the saguaro after Carnegie was likely a political decision that certainly did not hurt their chances of getting a grant.